Dropshipping for Beginners

Learn How To Build Your Own Dropshipping Business And Start Making Passive Income Today

By Robert J. Murphy

Copyright © 2017

Table of Contents

Introduction..1
Chapter 1..4
The Essentials of Dropshipping....................................4
Benefits of Dropshipping..9
Disadvantages of Dropshipping..............................11
Why you need to consider the dropshipping option..17
Chapter 2..**22**
Setting Up Your Dropshipping Business in 7 Days..22
Day 1: Identify Your Niche..23
Day 2: Look For and Contact Potential Suppliers..24
Day 3: Establish Your Brand....................................25
Day 4: Set Up Your Store...26
Day 5: Identify Products to Sell, Pricing, and Product Pages..27
Day 6: Finalize Your Set Up and Launch..................28
Day 7: Advertising and Promotion.........................30
Choosing the Best Dropshipping Platform................30
Chapter 3..**34**
The Dropshipping Supply Chain...............................34
Chapter 4..**40**
Searching for Wholesale Suppliers............................40
How to Find a Dropshipping Supplier.......................40
How to Spot Fake Dropshipping Suppliers.................42
Here are five things to look out for: 43
Difference Between Dropshipping Wholesaler and Manufacturer...44
Chapter 5..**46**
Choosing and Pricing Your Products........................46
Defining Your Products..46

Here are some factors to consider when choosing which products to sell:.. 47

How to Price Your Products.....................................48

Chapter 6...**50**

Success Tips for a New Dropshipping Business.............50

Customer Service Tips..50

Tips for Optimizing Shipping Costs..............................52

Tips for Improving Your Margins.................................53

Chapter 7...**55**

Some of the Top Dropshipping Firms............................55

Bonus...**63**

Have the Right Mindset...62

Conclusion...**64**

Introduction

I want to thank you and congratulate you for purchasing this book, *Dropshipping for Beginners: Learn How to Build Your Own Dropshipping Business and Start Making Passive Income Today.*

This book contains proven steps and strategies on how to start your very own dropshipping business from the comfort of your home. If you have been searching for a simple guide that contains step-by-step, actionable instructions, then this book is perfect for you.

There is no doubt regarding the wave of dropshipping businesses that are coming up every day. What is fueling this popularity? Well, dropshipping is a very easy and lucrative business service. It is a simple way to use the resources you have available to start and succeed in your very own entrepreneurial activity.

So what does this book offer you?

This book will teach you about the basic aspects of dropshipping, how it works, and everything you need to do to succeed in your new business.

In chapter one, you will learn how to define dropshipping, its basic structure, and some of its advantages and disadvantages. After that, I will show you how you can establish your own dropshipping business within a mere 7 days! Yes, it is possible! But you need the right guidance and information, and this book guarantees you that.

In chapter three, we cover how to find the best dropshipping wholesalers, and I show you some of the key signs of a fake supplier. Believe me, you do not want to waste time and money being conned by a scam artist.

Chapter four looks at how to choose the right products to sell. This is a critical factor in the success of your business. Do not assume that you will waltz into the market and dominate. You have to position yourself well; otherwise, you will be closing up shop pretty quickly.

In the final chapter, I share some of the best-kept tips that every seasoned dropshipper is aware of. Do you want to ensure that you make good margins?

Thanks again for downloading this book, I hope you enjoy it!

Chapter 1

The Essentials of Dropshipping

In this chapter, you will learn about some of the basic aspects of dropshipping as a business. We will discuss what dropshipping is all about, including an overview of how it works, its structure, and its benefits and disadvantages. It is important that you start your dropshipping venture on the right foot by understanding the essentials. This will enable you to establish yourself better as you move on in the future.

What is Dropshipping?

Dropshipping is the process of selling goods to customers through your e-commerce website without actually buying or storing any inventory yourself. It is a business model where you partner with a wholesaler who will fulfill your customer's orders. The wholesaler will receive orders from you and then process and deliver the products to your customers. You will not get to view or handle the products. The dropshipping partner is the one who handles the products and ships them to your customers.

Dropshipping can also be defined as a retail fulfillment process where you do not purchase any stock that you are selling. Instead, you sell products that belong to a third party. A customer places an order at your store, and you then send the order to your dropshipping partner to be processed. The items bought will be packaged and shipped out to your customer directly from the vendor's warehouse.

The best way to understand dropshipping is to compare it with a regular retail business.

In a regular business, you have a physical structure, maybe a warehouse or a shop, where you store the products that you intend to sell. You contact a wholesaler or manufacturer and order some products so that you can have inventory ready, just in case someone comes along and wants to buy from you.

If a customer comes along and makes an order, you process the order, package the product, and then deliver it to them. As the business owner, you essentially handle everything yourself.

Compare dropshipping retail and regular retail enterprises

Both of these enterprises are designed to accomplish the same purpose which is to sell products to customers. The major difference in these two models is that a regular retail outlet purchases inventory and keeps stocks of products while the dropshipping business does not invest in inventory and does not keep any stock.

Dropshipping business will only purchase goods when a customer places an order. Therefore, such a business does not need resources to invest in stock. Products are also paid for once a customer pays. The order is then fulfilled by a third party, in this case, the dropshipping partner firm.

Once the order is received, it is sent to the dropshipping warehouse where it will be processed, packaged and shipped out to the customer. However, it will have the retailer's address, so the customer will know the product is from the retailer's website.

How It Works

As the retailer, you do not need to have a brick-and-mortar structure. You can just have a website where you promote specific products. When a potential customer visits your online store, they have no idea that you do not own the inventory you are showing on the website. However, this does not matter because by then, you have already established a relationship with a wholesaler as well as a dropshipping company.

When the customer makes an online order, you take that order and inform the dropshipping company. The dropshipping company then goes to the wholesaler who stocks the product, picks up the order, packs it, and delivers it to the customer.

So how do you make money from this process?
When the customer makes the order, they also pay for the product. The dropshipping company will also charge you for the product and service they have provided. The difference between what you earn and what you are charged is your profit.
As you can see, you do not have to handle any inventory at all. You are basically fulfilling the customer's request and

providing a middleman service. This is something that you can do from your house and earn passive income.

Summary

Regular retail store selling products directly to customers

- Retail store owner orders goods regularly from suppliers

- The goods are kept in storage or display awaiting customer orders

- Once orders are placed, they are processed, packaged and shipped out to customers

The dropshipping process summary

- An entrepreneur advertises goods on their website

- Customers visit the website and buy the goods that they see

- The entrepreneur passes on the orders to a dropshipping partner for processing

Benefits of Dropshipping

Now that you have a basic overview of how the process works, let's look at some of the benefits of running your own dropshipping business:

1. Low capital requirement – Dropshipping does not require a huge upfront investment to start. There is no need to spend thousands of dollars stocking inventory in some warehouse. You will only buy a product from the wholesaler when a customer makes an order to request a product.

2. Less risk – One of the risks of owning a physical store that stocks products is that if customers do not show up, you are stuck with thousands of dollars worth of inventory that is not moving. You may even be forced to sell your products at a loss. But when you do not own the inventory, you do not have to worry about things like shortages, overstocking, or shifts in trends.

3. Wide product range – Since you do not have to have physical possession of any product to sell it to customers, you can literally sell anything that you want. All you have to do is display the photos and descriptions of the wide variety of goods that are

available. You are not limited by niche at all. For example, you can sell handbags, power tools, shoes, as well as kitchen appliances. A wider product range means a wider customer base, and hopefully, more profits.

4. Greater scalability – When you run your own dropshipping business, you do not have to manually package and deliver every order as you would in a regular business. This makes it much easier for you to scale and grow your business because fulfilling 100 units of a product takes the same amount of work as 1000 units.

5. Freedom of location – A dropshipping business is location-independent. In other words, you can run the business from anywhere in the world, as long as you have a laptop, a power source, and a reliable internet connection.

6. Passive income – dropshipping business provides one of the best ways of earning a passive income. Many entrepreneurs operating this e-commerce model often put in very little work each day. Therefore, you can make money as you attend to other matters.

7. All work done by dropshipping partner – There is often very little work for the entrepreneur to do. This is because orders are often processed or executed almost entirely by the dropshipping partner. A business owner does very little work and is, therefore, free to attend to other businesses or even family matters and employment.

8. Eliminates handling risks – Since all the products are shipped directly from the dropshipping partner's warehouse to the customer, the risks of damages, mishandling, and wrong deliveries are minimized. This helps reduce losses arising from handling errors

Disadvantages of Dropshipping

Though dropshipping is an awesome way to start your own business from home, there are some drawbacks that you have to know about. Here is a list of some of the challenges you may face. This list is by no means exhaustive as each business is unique in many aspects:

1. A large number of competitors – This is possibly the biggest challenge your business will face. Since

dropshipping suppliers have made it very easy for people to access their products, many businesses are currently flooding the market trying to sell popular items. This presents a challenge to new entrepreneurs and those still trying to establish themselves.

2. Lack of brand control – As a dropshipping retailer, you never get to come into contact with the products that your customer receives. This means that you will not have any control over your own brand. In other words, if the customer has a negative experience with the product for one reason or another, they will perceive your business negatively, yet you did not even touch the product.

3. Low margins – The truth is that most products that are drop shipped tend to generate minimal margins; usually around 20 percent. Once you subtract overheads, advertising, and other costs, you are left with a very small percentage margin. This means that you have to sell a lot of products just to make a decent profit. If you also consider the fact that you are also competing with the manufacturer and larger retailers, things become difficult.

4. Best niches are all taken – Success in the dropshipping business requires you to carefully select a lucrative niche market whose products are in high demand and trusted by customers. However, most dropshipping entrepreneurs complain that most of the great niches are all taken and even crowded. This causes them to choose niches that are not lucrative, and this affects the performance of the business. But even then, business experts do not wholly agree. They are of the opinion that a hardworking and enterprising business owner who markets his products well and puts in the hard work can overcome the niche problem.

5. Ease of starting: Sometimes the ease with which one can start a dropshipping enterprise causes challenges to genuine entrepreneurs. Investors without passion or interest tend to startup dropshipping businesses because it is easy to do so. They end up causing problems with suppliers and customers. They are the reason why dropshipping wholesalers charge monthly fees and demand a minimum quantity order. This is in the hope of weeding out all fake dropshipping retailers.

6. Hard work – While dropshipping is a relatively simple business to operate, it does require a lot of hard work, especially in the initial stages. You need to advertise, market your products, respond to queries, and write product descriptions and so much more. It is not easy work, but it is definitely worth it for dedicated entrepreneurs.

Is Dropshipping For Me?

There are some types of entrepreneurs that are a good fit for a dropshipping model while there are others that simply are not. Here are the entrepreneurs that fit this model:

- New entrepreneurs – If you have just started selling things online, then dropshipping is a great model for your business. Succeeding in e-commerce requires attracting a lot of traffic to your website and converting it into sales. Getting this right usually takes a long time. With dropshipping, you can start selling on a small scale even as you learn more about traffic optimization and conversion.

- Budget entrepreneurs – Since it does not require a lot of capital to start, dropshipping is perfect for entrepreneurs who do not have a large budget or want to maintain low startup costs. If you have limited capital and lack the resources to fully stock a retail store, then this model is definitely designed with you in mind.

- Validating entrepreneurs – If you are interested in selling a product that is new in the market or even set up a startup, dropshipping allows you to test the market without pumping too much money into inventory. You get to validate whether it is worth investing.

- Variety entrepreneurs – Entrepreneurs who want to sell a wide variety of products are adopting a dropshipping model. You will not have to spend a lot of money upfront on a wide range of inventory products. You are also free to partner with more than one dropshipping supplier. Many entrepreneurs prefer having two, three or more partners to have options and alternatives in the course of trade.

On the other hand, there are some forms of entrepreneurs that do not fit the dropshipping model. They include:

- Entrepreneurs focused on margins – Margins tend to be quite slim in the dropshipping business. They are usually about 10 to 20 percent. After paying for credit card fees, email service fees, app fees and shopping cart fees, you may only be left with a profit margin of a few percent. If margins are your focus, leave dropshipping alone.

- Entrepreneurs focused on brand-building – We all know how hard and long it takes to build a respected brand. However, the dropshipping business makes it even harder to do so. The reason for this is simple. You have no control over the customer experience! For example, a customer makes an order, and when you contact the dropshipping wholesaler, they tell you that it is out of stock. This can put you in a bind as you try to coordinate things, thus giving the customer a poor impression of your business. Another issue is that if the product may be delivered late or in bad condition, and it is your business, not the dropshipper, that will be perceived in a negative light.

Why you need to consider the dropshipping option

Dropshipping is basically one of the best e-commerce models that work and is popular with entrepreneurs. Traders are passionate about dropshipping because it is a model that is easy to start and provides a reliable method of earning passive income. With no requirement to invest huge amounts in stock and inventory, this business model is sustainable in the long term. It negates the need to rent out a brick and mortar store.

Since capital requirements are low, dropshipping stores can afford a wide array of goods. Customers love stores that have a wide variety of products and those that have fast shipping times. Most dropshippers offer immediate shipping and a variety of products. These will make customers happy and ensure that they keep coming back.

Running your own dropshipping business is a great idea, and you now have a good understanding of what you are getting yourself into. Can you make a good profit from this business and generate passive income from home? Absolutely! However, you should also consider the benefits and disadvantages mentioned above. You should also look at whether it is the right business for you.

In the next chapter, you will learn more about a dropshipping business and how you can get started.

Factors to consider when starting a dropshipping enterprise

Dropshipping is a very cost effective way of starting a web-based business. It provides an effective model of conducting retail business for a passive income for many years to come. As an entrepreneur, you get to own a virtual store where customers come and purchase products that they need then the orders are processed by a different entity which is your dropshipping partner.

Consider getting into a suitable niche market

To be a successful online entrepreneur, you need to get into a niche market. It may not matter much, but it is advisable to choose a field that you have a passion for and then search for the most marketable niches, whose goods regularly sell on popular platforms. A niche market, for instance, would be rear brake lights for the older Ford Mustang model,

Consider low volume, highly profitable niches

If you want to stand out from the crowd, then avoid the niches that everyone seems to choose. This creates unnecessary competition which may be unhealthy. Instead, choose items that sell low volumes but go for higher prices. While your volume of sales may be low to start with, you will receive much higher profits and ward of competition from other dropshipping retailers.

Basic steps to follow to achieve success as a dropshipping entrepreneur

There are certain steps that you can follow to become successful in the dropshipping sector. If you diligently follow these steps, then you will well be on your way to setting up a successful business

- Identify a suitable supplier and dropshipping fulfillment partner

- Identify the best selling products within a given niche area

- Organize your paperwork such as licenses, permits, etc., depending on your state

- Choose your preferred retail platform

- Proceed to prepare then manage your chosen listings

How to identify bestselling products

This step should be one of your initial steps. Identifying the best selling products is an important process as it can determine the success or otherwise of your business. If you can successfully execute this step and identify a suitable product to sell, then success will knock on your door a lot sooner than you think.

Use online search services: You should use online search services to identify products in niches that are popular and sell widely. Consider checking out market research labs that can help with the research bit. All you need to do is enter a name into the software, and it will provide you with all the metrics of the product such as mean selling price and cost of shipping.

You may also use the eBay completed listing method. This is a tried-and-tested method that works. Also, eBay is the most successful online market platform so any product doing well here is likely to do well on other platforms.

Another important step that you need to consider is to get your paperwork and documentation in order. Sometimes it is easy to ignore this if your e-commerce business is home based. However, your paperwork is important and getting it right from the onset is essential.

Acquiring documentation is really simple especially in the U.S. or Canada. Just check with your local council what documentation you will need. U.S. and Canadian residents need to get a tax ID. It is sometimes referred to as a vendor's license or a reseller's license.

Chapter 2

Setting Up Your Dropshipping Business in 7 Days

In this chapter, you will learn how to set up your very own dropshipping business in just seven days. This information will guide you through the dropshipping process by highlighting every single thing that a dropshipping entrepreneur like you needs to know and do.

The goal here is to help you start your business as quickly as possible instead of dragging you through many complex steps that will probably just waste your time. These steps indicated below have been simplified as much as possible.

So are you ready to begin?

Day 1: Identify Your Niche

Being passionate about starting your own business is awesome, but you need to start doing the hard and boring work from day one. This is important because you do not want to be engaging in a business that does not have a market or one that has too many competitors. This means you have to do some research. Here are some of the steps:

1. Brainstorm some niche ideas – You need to focus on a particular niche, especially one you are passionate about. Catering for a smaller subset of the market, e.g., CrossFit fans, vegetarians, or yoga lovers will help you create a business that can meet customer needs easily.

2. Run a Google Keyword Planner search – This tool will help you know how many searches people are conducting about a particular niche. This is how you know which products are popular.

3. Run an Amazon search – This will also help you identify which products are in great demand.

4. Conduct social media research – Use Facebook, YouTube, Twitter, or Reddit to see how your potential customers are interacting with your niche market. Also, identify influencers who have large audiences/followers in your niche.

5. Pick a niche – Use the data you have collected to decide which niche market you want to create a business around. Keep the rest of the data as a backup in case your chosen niche does not work out.

Day 2: Look For and Contact Potential Suppliers

Now you have to search for a dropshipper who can supply products for your business. It is possible that there may not be any suppliers for your niche product, but since you still have the backup list of niche ideas, you have options.

This step involves using Google search operators, which is an advanced way of conducting searches. This whole process is explained in detail in Chapter 3.

Day 3: Establish Your Brand

You need to do this early on so that your brand becomes the compass for your business. Here are some of the things you need to consider:

1. Choose a name for your brand – This will help customers identify your business.

2. Think of a tagline – Your tagline should be a summary of the unique value proposition of your business. For example, "Just Do It" is the tagline for Nike. It tells you what the company offers – the ability to achieve any sports feat when you wear their shoes.

3. Make a logo – This is a visual representation of your brand. You can make one yourself using templates from www.creativemarket.com.

4. Pick a color pallet – You need to make sure that every aspect of your website and products are consistent, especially the colors. You want to create a specific atmosphere and vibe on your website, so pick the colors wisely. Grasshoper.com can help you with this.

5. Set up your About Us page – This is the page that most visitors go to when they want to know more

about you. Tell people your brand story so that they can identify with your business. Your brand story is what persuades people to buy from you. It makes them think about what their lives would be like without you and how your products will transform their lives. Your brand story should go beyond the About Us page and into your social media accounts, adverts, and even customer support.

Day 4: Set Up Your Store

One of the best pieces of advice that every beginner should get is to avoid trying to make their store look perfect. There will always be something that needs to be improved, so if you wait until things look perfect, you will never launch your business. Here are a few steps to follow:

• Choose a platform – There are various e-commerce platforms that you can use in your dropshipping business. There are some critical factors that you have to consider, for example, how the platform integrates with your software, functionality and design requirements, etc. You can either go with an open-source platform like Magento or WooCommerce, or hosted platforms like BigCommerce and Shopify. More information on how to choose platforms is provided at the end of this chapter.

- Install a theme - This involves picking the layout and look of your online store. Some themes come at a price while others are free.

- Set up the store – This is where you now edit the colors, images, logo, fonts, menus, etc.

Day 5: Identify Products to Sell, Pricing, and Product Pages

Once you are happy with your store's appearance, you then need to determine the kind of products you will be selling. You will have to identify the specific products, their prices, and create product pages. You may be asking why this particular step was not done before launching the website.

The truth is that most suppliers need some time before they get back to you, and this may delay setting up your accounts. Secondly, it is best to set up the visuals of your store so that you end up choosing products that are a good fit for your brand.

You need to take time when pricing the products you sell in your store. The cost of products in your store is crucial because each niche is very competitive. There are plenty of other entrepreneurs doing the same thing you are doing and selling the same product.

However, you should not undercut yourself because this will affect profitability and your income. There is a delicate balance that you need to strike. Even then, great marketing skills, good quality products, top notch customer service and other interpersonal skills that you apply can help you maintain a reasonable price and still attract customers.

For more information regarding how to choose products to sell and the relevant pricing, go to Chapter 4.

Day 6: Finalize Your Set Up and Launch

You have already done everything necessary to set up your dropshipping business and the only thing left is to launch. Your online store is not perfect, and it may take a while for you to achieve your dream of becoming a millionaire, but at least you will be earning some passive income.

Here are some of the final touches that you need to add:

1. Create social media accounts for your store on Facebook, Pinterest, Instagram, Twitter, etc. Social media accounts are very important for marketing purposes and for interacting with your customers.

2. Install the relevant apps – You need some apps to improve customer experience and sales efficiency. Just make sure that you do not overload your store with apps since this may make your website run slower. Some great apps include Privy, Cross-sells, Trust, Yotpo, and others.

3. Install Google Analytics – You need to monitor the number of site visitors, purchases, and signups. Measuring customer data is critical to online business success.

4. Test the system – Try purchasing to see what problems there might be and get a feel of user experience. Confirm the Add Cart button, checkout funnel, and email confirmation are all functioning as required.

5. Launch – Your online dropshipping store is now ready! All you have to do now is do away with the password protection that you had set up on your website. You can do this by going to Online Store > Themes > Preferences and then scroll down the page. Uncheck the box that says Password Protect Your Storefront. Go ahead and send out tweets, Facebook posts, and emails to your contacts to generate traffic to your store.

Day 7: Advertising and Promotion

There are three ways to attract visitors and potential customers. These are:

- Search engine optimization (SEO)

- Facebook ads

- Content marketing

Choosing the Best Dropshipping Platform

On Day 4 of setting up your store, you have to choose a platform. This can be very difficult for someone who has never done any kind of online business. However, there are some factors that can guide you. Consider the following:

- Whether the platform allows you to send orders to several different suppliers.

- Whether the platform can integrate with your dropshipping software.

- Whether the platform has the specific design and technical requirements required by your dropshipping suppliers.

Once you have considered these factors, you then have to determine whether you want to set up your store on an Open Source platform or a Hosted platform.

Open Source software is free to use and is supported by a community of web developers who create extensions and plug-ins. Apart from the minimal cost of setting up your e-commerce website, open source software also allows greater flexibility, that is, you can alter the code to get your site to do whatever you want. However, there are hidden costs for maintaining the code, and you are ultimately responsible for hosting the code. Examples of Open Source platforms include:

- Magento - It is a very flexible platform that has numerous extensions and is generally very affordable. However, it is also one of the more expensive open source software in terms of coding, hosting and development costs. Still, Magento is one of the best free platforms for e-commerce, and you may want to consider it over others.

- WooCommerce – It is hosted on the Wordpress platform, which means it has a huge number of developers, a large plug-in repository, and is cheap and sophisticated. It is the most popular e-commerce platform on the market at the moment.

Hosted platforms are also popular because you do not have to worry about where to host your server or code. You pay a fee so that the platform maintains everything for you; all you have to focus on is marketing your business. However, there is less flexibility in terms of the apps you can use. The host platform only allows you to use apps that are customized for its platform. Examples include:

- Shopify – This intuitive platform is growing fast in popularity due to great functionalities and features.

- BigCommerce – It offers nested sub-categories, unlike Shopify, and provides support for wholesale suppliers.

There you have it! That is basically all you need to know to set up and launch your dropshipping business in just one week. In the next chapter, you will learn how to identify credible wholesale dropshippers.

Chapter 3

The Dropshipping Supply Chain

In business, there is the supply chain management. This term stands for the entire process that a product takes from its initial concept stage to production, transportation, storage or warehousing until the product reaches the end consumer who is the customer.

If you are interested in the dropshipping business model, then you need to be well acquainted with the dropshipping supply chain process. For our purposes, we shall focus more on three essential components. These include;

- The manufacturer

- The wholesaler

- The retail shop

Manufacturers are the originators of the goods that you will sell as a dropshipping retailer. In most cases, you will not directly interact with the supplier because they sell their produce in bulk to wholesalers and suppliers. Manufacturers often don't sell directly to suppliers.

Wholesalers buy their stock directly from the manufacturer. They buy in bulk and at a lower price. They also sell the products in large quantities to retailers and suppliers. Wholesalers own large stores and warehouses where they store their wares. Many wholesalers operate within specific industries or niche sectors and store products from dozens of manufacturers.

Retailers are often not able to purchase goods directly from manufacturers, so they get their goods from wholesalers. Many manufacturers have minimum order requirements which retailers often cannot meet. They also lack large storage facilities and prefer small, regular purchases that they can afford.

Dropshipping entrepreneurs

Generally, dropshipping retailers are not part of the supply chain management. They are considered to be more of a service provider than anything else. Both retailers and wholesalers can provide dropshipping services. Manufacturers and warehousing experts sometimes partner with dropshipping firms to fulfill orders on their behalf.

As a dropshipper, you need to partner with the expert who is providing you with the best prices as well as the best service. If a manufacturer is willing to provide dropshipping fulfillment services, then partner with the firm. This makes it cheaper for you and you will not only attract more customers but also make more profits.

A look at the dropshipping process

Now let us say we have a dropshipping e-commerce site that sells mobile phone accessories. A lot of smartphone owners checkout our e-commerce website to view the various accessories available. There is a customer, sayMs. Naomi, who wishes to purchase a mobile phone charger for her smartphone.

So Ms. Naomi gets onto our website, places an order for a charger and pays for the order. Once her order is complete and in the system, a couple of processes will be triggered.

1. An order, complete with product specifications and shipping details, will be sent to our fulfillment company.

2. An email will be dispatched to the customer confirming the purchase, information about the payment and other essential details.

3. The dropshipping fulfillment company will receive payment depending on agreed payment mode. Many of them prefer to charge purchases to a credit card.

4. The fulfillment company then processes the order and ships out the specified mobile phone charger to Ms. Naomi's given address. The sender's address is indicated by our online retail outlet.

Funds will be deducted from our company account to pay for the product and shipping. The profit that we make is the difference in price between what we charge our customer Naomi and what we were charged for the same product.

One point worth noting is that we do not do any work regarding the order. All that we needed to do was confirm email sent to the customer, the order is sent to our fulfillment partner and a tracking number provided to the buyer, Ms. Naomi. This means that dropshipping is such a hands-off business that many consider it to be a source of passive income. Their main, and often only, responsibility us to maintain an inventory or list of products on the website and to dispatch orders made by customers. The rest of the work will be handled by the fulfillment firm.

Such orders are often processed within a matter of hours as soon as confirmation is received. This is in contrast to online retail outlets that sometimes take 24 hours or an entire day to process a simple order. It saves customers a lot oftime, and they get to receive their orders much faster than buying directly from regular retailers.

In essence, dropshipping companies are completely out of sight of customers. They simply fulfill an order placed by a customer. Customers such as Ms. Naomi will visit an e-commerce site like ours, buy goods from the website and pay on the website. They will have no idea that a dropshipping firm processed their order.

Chapter 4

Searching for Wholesale Suppliers

In this chapter, you will learn how to find good suppliers and how to identify the fake ones. A lot of newbies in the dropshipping business have been scammed by these fake wholesalers, so you need to know how to spot them.

How to Find a Dropshipping Supplier

- Use search operators – It is not easy to find suppliers online using standard Google searches. This is because they care more about manufacturing and distribution than SEO. Therefore, you need to use search operators to narrow down your search results. For example, if you want to sell skinny blue jeans, use search operators like:

  - Blue skinny jeans + wholesale

  - Blue skinny jeans + bulk

- Blue skinny jeans + dropshipping

- Blue skinny jeans + supplier

- Blue skinny jeans + inurl: dropshipping

- Use only a few keywords – Pick a few keywords and try different variations of them. Use Google Keyword Planner to get relevant keywords.

- Mix up your keywords – There is a Keyword Mixer Tool (www.keywordmixer.com) that you can use to identify all the variations of keywords that you need. The tool contains three columns: keywords, operators, and variations. You just fill in the first two columns; click Combine, and the tool will generate all the variations possible, which you then use to search for suppliers.

- Create an Excel/Google sheet – You will need to save the names, web addresses, email addresses, and phone numbers of the suppliers that you find during your searches. Make sure you also have a column for indicating whether you have contacted a particular supplier or not. This will help you stay organized.

- Begin your search – This may take hours. Ensure that you also go beyond just the first page of your Google results. Do not worry if a supplier has a website that is not pleasing to look at. Most of them are not keen on such aspects.

- Dig deeper into the search results – Once you have a list of potential dropshipping wholesalers, go to their websites and learn more about them.

- Reach out to the supplier – Send your preferred suppliers an email enquiring about their services. Once you have the relevant feedback from all the suppliers, make your choice.

- Open an account – For some wholesale suppliers, you can open an account on their website. They are going to ask for your Sales Tax ID or Resale License. If you do not already have one, then consult a lawyer to help you or seek online resources that may be cheaper.

How to Spot Fake Dropshipping Suppliers

By now you should be aware that your dropshipping supplier is extremely critical to the success of your business. This means you have to ensure that they can be trusted before you sign any document. Many fake dropshipping suppliers have caused many businesses to close prematurely.

Here are five things to look out for:

- A supplier who does not provide contact details – Be very careful when you visit the website of a supplier and they do not have multiple contact details, for example, phone numbers, email addresses, physical location, etc.

- A supplier who sells directly to consumers – A dropshipping supplier should only sell to dropshipping retailers (e-commerce websites) who do not store inventory. Anyone who sells directly to individual consumers is a fake because they are contravening the fundamental aspect of a dropshipping wholesaler.

- A supplier who does not provide sample products – You need to check the quality of the products during negotiations. If they refuse to send samples or ask for more time, they are probably a fake.

- A supplier who refuses to sign a contract – Anyone who does not want to enter a legally binding agreement is a fraud.

- A supplier who requests monthly membership fees – Genuine dropshipping wholesalers never charge fees to hold inventory. You only pay per order. If they ask for money to hold stock, they are a fake supplier.

Difference Between Dropshipping Wholesaler and Manufacturer

The process of finding a good dropshipping supplier is usually a bit cumbersome for beginners. This is because most people tend to use certain search terms interchangeably, and this generally causes some level of confusion. You need to realize that a dropshipping wholesaler and a manufacturer are two different things.

A manufacturer is a person or entity that actually makes the product you want to purchase. In some cases, the manufacturer may already have an established dropshipping program, and you can simply partner with them directly. This is usually a good idea since the lack of a middleman means you get a better price and generate higher profit margins.

A dropshipping wholesaler is a person or entity that buys products from a manufacturer and then delivers them to the customer on your behalf. There are times when a manufacturer may simply decide to focus on making the product instead of selling to small companies. This allows them to sell products in bulk to dropshipping wholesalers who the set up a dropshipping program. You, as the dropshipping retailer, then join the program.

Apart from these two terms, it is also important that you become familiar with a third term – a dropshipping aggregator. This is a wholesaler who has formed partnerships with hundreds of manufacturers and stocks their products in bulk. A dropshipping aggregator makes your life easier because partnering with them means you can market hundreds of different products in your store.

However, there is one challenge that you will face with an aggregator. They take a big chunk of your profit margin for providing you with their service. On top of that, they also charge an annual fee that may run into hundreds of dollars. For a dropshipping beginner, this may make it very hard to build your business. It is advised that you avoid dropshipping aggregators if you have just launched your dropshipping business.

In the next chapter, you will learn about how to choose products to sell.

Chapter 5

Choosing and Pricing Your Products

In this chapter, you will learn how to choose the best products possible to sell and the kind of pricing model you need to come up with to convince customers to buy from you.

Defining Your Products

The first thing you need to realize is that you cannot sell everything. You may have the luxury of not dealing with the headaches of inventory management, but if you want to set yourself apart from competitors, you must focus on a few specific products.

The important thing is to make sure that your products are aligned with the niche market you selected in Chapter 2. Sell a few relevant main products rather than many irrelevant accessories. This will help generate more traffic to your online store.

Customers are more likely to believe your brand story if you focus on a few items. If you provide them with ten or more different types of products, your brand story becomes less convincing, and customers get overwhelmed by all the options, and you will not make any sales.

Here are some factors to consider when choosing which products to sell:

- Choose a product that solves a problem

- Choose a product of high quality

- Choose a product that will generate good margins – Your goal should be to make 30+ percent gross profit.

- Choose a product that will sell well online – Avoid unreasonable items like expensive, heavy, or large products that require specialized customer service or unique shipping arrangements.

At the end of the day, it is all about intuition and strategy when choosing which products to sell.

How to Price Your Products

There are four factors you need to consider when defining your pricing:

- MSRP – This stands for Manufacturer Suggested Retail Price. It is the price proposed by a manufacturer so that customers find their product being sold at a similar price in different stores.

- MAP – This stands for Minimum Advertised Price. This is the least price that you are legally allowed to sell a product. It is meant to prevent price wars between retailers.

- Margin – This is the difference between the price you sold the product and how much you paid for it. A larger margin means more revenue and more money available to pay your business expenses.

- The price of your competitors – If other dropshipping businesses within your niche market are selling at lower prices, you will lose customers.

Most beginners use the MSRP pricing model because it is simpler to understand and allows you to make a reasonable profit. The problem is that your competition may be selling their products using the MAP model, thus attracting more customers. This is why you need to create a great brand story so that customers give you their loyalty.

In the next chapter, you will learn some of the critical tips that can make or break your business.

Chapter 6

Success Tips for a New Dropshipping Business

In this chapter, we take a look at some of the tips that can make your dropshipping business successful. As a new entrepreneur in the dropshipping sector, it is important that you know the things to do and those to avoid. You will learn a bit about handling customers, setting up your shipping costs, and improving your profit margin.

Customer Service Tips

If there is one key factor that will determine your success in the dropshipping business, then it has to be your reputation. It is important to give customers the best experience so that they trust you and stay loyal. Here are some best practices to remember:

- You are always responsible for everything that goes wrong. Even if the supplier messed up, you are the one the customer will blame. You need to step up and appease the customer, even if it means losing money. You do not want to risk getting negative reviews.

- Understand what customers want and need. Ensure a secure checkout system and keep their personal information protected. Make your website professional and user-friendly. If possible, provide customers with a way to track their order without having to contact you all the time.

- Be knowledgeable about your products. Create detailed product descriptions, FAQ pages, and even a newsletter to give customers access to more information. This will help you come across as an expert.

- Always keep your customers happy. Happy customers are repeat customers who go out and spread the word to others. Treat your customers well.

Tips for Optimizing Shipping Costs

When you launch your dropshipping business, you have to establish a proper shipping strategy. Your shipping charges will affect whether a customer completes a transaction or not. The problem you have is that you have no control over the actual shipping cost – the supplier does.

So what do you do?

You can find out what your competitors are charging and then you set up a standard shipping policy. Here are some strategies:

- Offer customers free shipping – Customers expect this nowadays. However, you can advertise "free" shipping and then add your shipping cost to the MSRP so that the customer pays for it anyway.

- Offer a flat rate – Group your products according to a particular weight and price range and then offer that entire range of products a flat rate for shipping. Once your sales improve, you can look at fast-moving product ranges and increase your shipping charges.

Tips for Improving Your Margins

Margins for a dropshipping business are tight. Wholesalers tend to charge extra costs to the product price because they are responsible for stocking the inventory, insuring it, packaging, and processing costs. This means they have to pass on that cost to you, the dropshipping retailer. Stiff competition also means you may have to offer customers lower prices, and this lowers your profit margin.

So how can you maximize your margins?

Here are some ideas:

- Avoid selling the same product as everybody else. Sounds obvious, right? You do not want to enter a market that is already saturated with other dropshippers. You will get lost in a sea of retailers who are lowering prices just to survive.

- Check out as many online selling platforms as possible. Go to Amazon, eBay, or Bonanzle and see how many sellers there are offering unique products. You may stumble upon a market gap to take advantage of.

- Avoid having back orders. Imagine if a customer makes an order for a product and after contacting the supplier, they inform you that the product is out of stock. You are now left with the task of explaining to the customer why you cannot fulfill their order. This is a back order, and it can lead to negative feedback and lost sales. To avoid this kind of scenario, you can decide to stock some items at home. In case of a back order, you sell your stock and then ask the supplier to send you the item when they have restocked. Alternatively, you should have a backup supplier in case the first supplier does not come through in time.

- Find a very specific niche instead of selling what everyone else is. For example, instead of selling smartphones, why not sell colorful phone cases for teens or tough cases for handymen?

All the tips provided in this chapter will come in handy when you are running your new dropshipping business. Keep them in mind, practice them, and you will stand a better chance of retaining customers and making better profit margins.

Chapter 7

Some of the Top Dropshipping Firms

The Dropshipping Concept

Entrepreneurs concur that dropshipping is generally one of the simplest yet most rewarding business models especially for new entrepreneurs who do not have experience or large investment capital. Some of the best platforms to establish such a business include Oberlo and Shopify. Dropshipping remains one of the best business models for new and low capital entrepreneurs even though it has its own fair share of challenges.

The basic idea behind dropshipping is that you, the entrepreneur, will contact and establish relationships with wholesale suppliers who provide dropshipping services. You should take your time to identify the most suitable dropshipping wholesale partners before signing an agreement. Check all the terms and conditions and make sure you understand each one of them and are happy with the entire document.

Now you will then need to identify the most suitable platform to establish your e-commerce dropshipping website. You can borrow images and product descriptions from your wholesale partner and use these for marketing and promotional purposes. You need visitors to come to your store and purchase products and keep coming back.

Ensure that you operate within a suitable niche. It will be up to you to find your preferred niche. You can base this on your passion or any field that you like. You may also choose to focus on a popular niche but be careful it is not overcrowded. A niche market can be PS4 computer games, Smartphone accessories, electronics, and so on. If you can master these few basics, then you understand the basic concept behind dropshipping.

A Look at Top Dropshipping Fulfillment Firms

Vista Wholesale

Vista is a large wholesale firm that has been providing fulfillment services on eBay since the early 1990s. Vista

Wholesale today provides dropshipping services to retail partners who sell to customers on eBay, Amazon and worldwide. The firm has a great program that enables willing partners to checkout the products available and the signup without paying any fees upfront.

SaleHoo

SaleHoo is an online firm that provides a platform for dropshippers, providing them with the necessary infrastructure, including a detailed directory of warehouse dropshippers who can partner with retail entrepreneurs on the dropshipping model. The SaleHoo site has plenty of tools that you can use to customize your e-commerce site. SaleHoo is popular with entrepreneurs because of its regularly updated blog where members get to read about the latest developments and also engage with each other.

Inventory Source

Another excellent dropshipping partner for new and existing retail sites is Inventory Source. This is a totally reliable partner with an accurate product list and all the essential information. As a dropshipper, you want to have an association with such a reliable partner. You will gain access to powerful software tools which ensure that you can easily identify a reliable supplier. There is a regular fee for some of the services while a free service is available for basic members.

Alibaba

Alibaba is one of the world's largest trade and e-commerce platforms. Its website, www.alibaba.com is one of the most popular on the internet. As a trader, you can find just about any product on this site. It is very popular with dropshippers, especially those who seek affordable products for their customers. The site has very affordable products of all kinds so entrepreneurs can find products they want here. The only challenge is the shipping time basically because of shipping times. Apparently, Alibaba is based in China so shipping times have to be taken into consideration.

Wholesale Central

Another reliable dropshipping partner is Wholesale Central. This organization's website comes with an efficient software tool that helps you search across different product categories such as Smartphone accessories, men's leather shoes and so much more. All the suppliers who provide these products are listed, making it easy for you to reach out to them. This provides you with convenience when identifying quality products for your store and partnering with suitable dropshipping firms.

Worldwide Brands

Worldwide Brands is essentially a complete directory of highly regarded dropshippers. On their website is a compilation of verified and certified wholesale suppliers. If you sign up for this firm, you can expect to engage positively with any of the listed firms. Once you find dropshipping partners that you believe are suitable, you will know for certain that these are reliable partners who can be relied upon to provide excellent services, quality products and great prices that you and your customers desire. You will then be able to place orders on behalf of your customers and have the orders fulfilled as required.

Dropship Direct

Yet another popular dropshipping partner is Dropship Direct. If you partner with this firm, then you will enjoy access to over 100,000 products all from more than 900 different brands. As a partner, you will be required to open a free account which allows you access to a database comprising hundreds of thousands of different products ranging from electronics to automobile parts and much more.

Sunrise Wholesale

Together with its partners, Sunrise Wholesale has access to warehousing and distribution centers measuring more than 600,000 square feet. Sunrise Wholesale is especially trusted for fast and accurate processing of customer orders. It has an A+ rating with the BBB, Better Business Bureau, indicating that it is a trustworthy firm to partner with. As a member, you can use the provided search tool to make queries and also get access to over 15000 products and brands.

Mega Goods

Mega Goods is a dropshipping services organization and a direct supplier. Through its simplified website which is very easy for entrepreneurs to use, the firm makes dropshipping a very easy and convenient process. This particular firm deals mostly with electronic goods such as kitchen appliances, television sets, steam irons and so on. You can find goods on this site from more than 45 various categories. As a dropshipper, you will definitely appreciate the wide variety of goods available, speedy processing of orders and the 30-day free trial and a $14.99 monthly subscription.

Bonus

Have the Right Mindset

Dropshipping, although being an online business, is still a business and as such should be treated, 50% of a business's success is determined by the mindset of the owner, here is a list of 6 key points that you have to keep in mind while you build and run your dropshipping business:

- Purpose: It must always be clear to you why you have decided to start this business because that is the only way you will be able to face the difficult times and always get out victorious. When difficult appears you must be ready and be enough motivated to overcome them.

- Rock Solid: Always think about the purpose of setting up your business. This term means that you must be like a rock in the ocean, even if it encounters extensive battering from waves (similar to difficulties) it remains solid and unshaken.

- Kaizen: This is a Japanese word that means continuous improvement, and it's the philosophy that you have to apply to your business

- Process Oriented: You must focus your attention on the process of managing your business because once you learn to handle the business and its challenges, then your business will most definitely become profitable and successful

- Belief: Before your business is well-known and successful have to believe in it

- Quality and Contribution: the first goal of activity is not to generate profits but to create value for its customers if you can do this you will not only generate profits, but customers will also be happy to buy from you

So if you follow these six steps, you will already be halfway to create a successful business not only online but also offline

Conclusion

Thank you again for purchasing this book!

I hope this book was able to help you to learn all you need to know to launch your very own dropshipping business. If you have been considering whether this is the right business to help you earn some passive income, now you know.

The next step is to actually start doing the work necessary to set up your business. It will not do you any good to read this book and not take action. Go to Chapter 2 and read the seven steps that can help you start your business within one week. Start researching which niche market to go into and move on from there. It is very fulfilling knowing that you are making money from home and earning a decent income online.

Finally, if you enjoyed this book, then I'd like to ask you for a favor, would you be kind enough to leave a review for this book on Amazon? It'd be greatly appreciated!

Click here to leave a review for this book on Amazon! Thank you and good luck!

– Robert J. Murphy

www.ingramcontent.com/pod-product-compliance
Lightning Source LLC
Chambersburg PA
CBHW071233220526
45468CB00002B/829